Tell Me About It

Anne Montgomery

One is soft.

One is hard.

One is wet.

One is dry.

One is hot.

One is cold.

One is **rough**.

One is smooth.

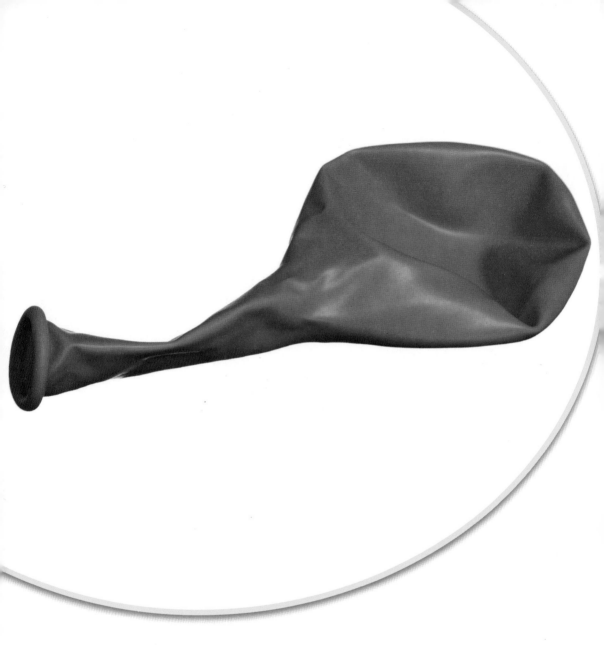

One is **flat**.

One is round.

One is fast.

One is slow.

One is young.

One is old.

One is big.

One is small.

Let's Do Science!

How can you describe things like a scientist? Try this!

What to Get

❏ 3 things you can hold and look at, such as an apple, a twig, or an eraser
❏ paper and pencil

What to Do

1 Make a chart like this one. Write the names of the three things you chose.

		1
Item	Sight 👁	Touch ✋
apple 🍎		
twig		
eraser		

2 Hold each thing, one at a time. Write how it looks under 👁 . Write how it feels under ✋ .

3 Describe how the things are the same. Describe how they are different.

Glossary

flat—having a wide and smooth surface

rough—having a surface that is not smooth

Index

big, 16

cold, 7

dry, 5

fast, 12

flat, 10

hard, 3

hot, 6

old, 15

rough, 8

round, 11

slow, 13

small, 17

smooth, 9

soft, 2

wet, 4

young, 14

Your Turn!

Look at this mug of hot chocolate. Describe it every way you can.

Consultants

Sally Creel, Ed.D.
Curriculum Consultant

Leann Iacuone, M.A.T., NBCT, ATC
Riverside Unified School District

Jill Tobin
California Teacher of the Year
Semi-Finalist
Burbank Unified School District

Publishing Credits

Conni Medina, M.A.Ed., *Managing Editor*
Lee Aucoin, *Creative Director*
Diana Kenney, M.A.Ed., NBCT, *Senior Editor*
Lynette Tanner, *Editor*
Lexa Hoang, *Designer*
Hillary Dunlap, *Photo Editor*
Rachelle Cracchiolo, M.S.Ed., *Publisher*

Image Credits: p.23 FoodPhotogr Eising/age fotostock; p.2 iStock; pp.18–19 (illustrations) J.J. Rudisill; all other images from Shutterstock.

Library of Congress Cataloging-in-Publication Data

Montgomery, Anne (Anne Diana), author.
 Tell me about it / Anne Montgomery,
  pages cm
  Summary: "It is time to learn how to describe things."—
Provided by publisher.
  Audience: K to grade 3.
  Includes index.
  ISBN 978-1-4807-4526-1 (pbk.) —
  ISBN 978-1-4807-5135-4 (ebook)
 1. Science—Methodology—Juvenile literature.
 2. Observation (Scientific method)—Juvenile literature.
 3. Readers (Primary) I. Title.
  Q175.2.M65 2015
  507.2—dc23
                                    2014008625

Teacher Created Materials

5301 Oceanus Drive
Huntington Beach, CA 92649-1030
http://www.tcmpub.com
ISBN 978-1-4807-4526-1